HOME ECONOMICS
The Consequences of Changing Family Structure

HOME ECONOMICS
The Consequences of Changing Family Structure

Nick Schulz

AEI Press
Washington, D.C.

Distributed by arrangement with the Rowan & Littlefield Publishing Group, 4501 Forbes Boulevard, Suite 200, Lanham, MD 20706. To order call toll free 1-800-462-6420 or 1-717-794-3800.

For all other inquiries please contact AEI Press, 1150 17th Street, N.W., Washington, D.C. 20036 or call 1-800-862-5801.

Schulz, Nick, 1972–
  Home economics : the consequences of changing family structure / Nick Schulz.
    pages cm.
  Includes bibliographical references.
  ISBN 978-0-8447-7260-8 (pbk.) -- ISBN 0-8447-7260-7 (pbk.)
  ISBN 978-0-8447-7261-5 (ebook) -- ISBN 0-8447-7261-5 (ebook)
  1. Family demography--United States. 2. Families--Economic aspects--United States. 3. United States--Economic conditions.
  4. Economics--Sociological aspects. I. Title.
  HQ759.98.S38 2013
  306.850973--dc23

CONTENTS

ACKNOWLEDGMENTS

I'd like to thank Arthur Brooks, David Gerson, and the rest of the men and women of the American Enterprise Institute who care so much for the future of the country they love. I'd like to thank the William Simon Foundation for its indispensable support for this project. I'd like to thank Greg Lane, Karin Agness, and the staff of the American Enterprise Institute's Values & Capitalism project for their encouragement, and American.com's Ellie Bartow for her wise edits. Three anonymous reviewers provided cogent comments on the first draft; I have adopted many of their suggestions, and the book is very much the better as a result. I'd like to thank Bill and Lynne Schulz, Charlie and Andrea Murphy, and other relatives who have taught me through word and deed the importance of home and kinship. Lastly, I'd like to thank Lauren, Olivia, Ryan, and Gwen for showing me that a family is a treasure nothing short of a miracle.

1

ECONOMICS AND THE CRISIS OF THE FAMILY

Economics–from the greek, 'oikos' for home, and 'nomia' for management

"The first thing to understand about the present crisis of the family is that it did not materialize overnight."

—Christopher Lasch[1]

This project was born out of frustration.

For several years I have been researching and writing about economics and economic policy. In 2010, I copublished a popular book on modern economic growth and the important role that institutions—laws, norms, culture, entrepreneurship, and so on—play in successful economies and material abundance.[2]

I have also edited thousands of articles on economic topics over the years and have had even more conversations with policymakers, politicians, business leaders, and intellectuals about economics—everything from income inequality to trade to tax policy to immigration and beyond.

Over time it became increasingly clear that something important was often missing from the broader public discussion of economics and economic outcomes: the effects of enormous changes to the structure of American family life over the last half century. In particular, what's missing from discussions of economic policy and politics is serious consideration of the economic consequences of changing family structure, particularly the increasing frequency of out-of-wedlock birth.

I come to this project as someone who writes primarily about economics and not primarily about social and cultural issues, but I also have found it impossible to write about economic topics without reference to some dramatic social shifts.

This book will advance a few related arguments. First, the collapse of the intact family is one of the most significant economic facts of our time. The discussion of the family is often tied up in culture war politics—debates about feminism, gay marriage, birth control, abortion, and the like. Those are important and interesting topics. But because the debate about family structure is so thoroughly tied up in the culture war, those who think of themselves as primarily interested in economic topics—business media, corporate leaders, Treasury and Commerce secretaries, macroeconomists, and so on—often avoid this subject.

Second, while intact families have always been economically significant, I will argue that they may be more important than ever. Their heightened importance has to do with the changing nature of the American economy.

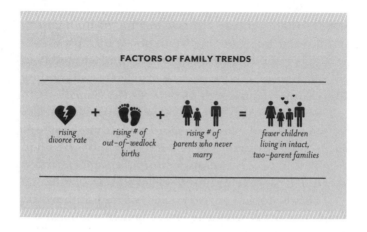

FACTORS OF FAMILY TRENDS

rising divorce rate + rising # of out-of-wedlock births + rising # of parents who never marry = fewer children living in intact, two-parent families

Crudely put, the American economy continues to shift from one built upon brawn to one built upon brains and social skills. Consider that in 1900 over 40 percent of Americans worked on farms, many performing mostly unskilled labor.[3] By 1930 the percentage of farmers had dropped to a little over 20 percent of the population. Today fewer than 2 percent of Americans live on farms and much modern farming and agriculture production is highly technology intensive.[4]

A similar transformation is happening in American manufacturing. The percentage of Americans working in manufacturing jobs that require little education, skill, or training is much smaller than it was in the middle of the twentieth century. While it ballooned to almost 20 percent of total employment in the 1960s, today it is down to 10 percent.[5]

Manufacturing jobs today, as with agriculture, often require the use of sophisticated technology and the ability to learn and adapt in a dynamic environment. Such an environment relies much less on physical prowess and much more on softer capacities such as education, willingness to learn and solve problems, and useful social and personality skills.

Meanwhile, America's service economy keeps growing, requiring a different set of skills for an individual to succeed. High-growth sectors of the economy in the future include health care and education. These sectors are increasingly technology intensive and require the steady and ongoing accumulation of knowledge and social skills.

However crude this characterization of the changing nature of the American economy, it is a helpful framework for asking what economic relevance the family has today and is likely to have in the future.

My own research and writings in recent years have primarily focused on technology and entrepreneur-led growth. Like many people who think about the economy, I considered the debates over family structure a cultural issue distinct from economic issues. But over time this bifurcated view became untenable.

I found it became impossible to speak intelligently about, say, income inequality without discussing changing family structure (as well as technology and trade). It became difficult to discuss depressed wages for low-skilled workers without also bringing out-of-wedlock birth rates among lower-class white Americans into the picture. It was challenging to talk about entrepreneur-led growth and not include the rates of entrepreneurial risk-taking among those raised in intact families and those who were not.

This book will establish what has happened to family structure over the last half century and ruminate on the causes of those changes. It will also discuss what we can reasonably say we know about the economic consequences of the changes in family.

To the best of my ability I will do this without passing judgment about divorce or out-of-wedlock births. Not because I do not have strong feelings about these issues, but because this book is predicated upon the belief that discussing these issues exclusively in moral terms is part of what has turned many people off from wanting to discuss the centrality of family structure to economic outcomes.

There are perfectly good reasons for the desire to avoid talking about the changes to the American family. Everyone either is or knows and has a deep personal connection to a person who is divorced, cohabiting, or gay; or who has had a child out-of-wedlock; or had an abortion; and so on. Great numbers of people simply want to avoid awkward talk of what are seen as primarily personal issues or issues of individual morality.

Another reason for the squeamishness about discussing changing family structure can be found in the bruising debate over the Moynihan Report, which I will discuss later in the book. For a variety of reasons, public discussions of family structure in the United States quickly became inextricably tied up with the country's often bitter politics of race, feminism, and sexual politics. Over time, many Americans felt it was safer to avoid talking about family structure because doing so meant talking about a suite of contentious and uncomfortable political issues.

One thing I seek to illuminate is the way concerns about the family, while originally tangled with America's racial politics, have now moved well beyond concerns about race. While Daniel Patrick Moynihan was writing about problems in "The Negro Family" in the 1960s, his concerns apply to Hispanic and white Americans today.

The writer Amanda Marcotte made an interesting comment about social scientists who point out declining rates of marriage and rising rates of divorce. She said many of them want to "restore the patriarchy to a perceived '50s-era heyday."[6]

While I will discuss marriage and divorce, my intent is not to restore some earlier period of American history and social arrangements. Nostalgia is not generally a good basis for thinking constructively about the world.

This book instead is designed to discuss a different kind of what I call "Home Ec": facts about changes in family life and their economic consequences. In so doing, we can broaden the public discussion of economic outcomes so they better reflect reality.

If it is helpful to the reader, take as my operating assumption that I do not care whether people divorce or have kids outside of marriage. I simply want to establish commonly agreed-upon benchmarks so we can say what we know about the economic outcomes related to family structure.

If successful, this book will make people more comfortable discussing some of the basic facts about the economic consequences of the family, no matter their political leanings.

2

WHAT DO WE KNOW ABOUT CHANGING FAMILY STRUCTURE?

"The process of making human beings human is breaking down in America."

—James Coleman[7]

The American family has changed dramatically over the last half century. For example, in 1960 about 75 percent of adults (those ages 18 and over) were married. In 2011, for the first time, fewer than 50 percent of households were made up of married couples.[8]

This and other developments in American family life prompted *The Economist* magazine to remark that "The iconic American family, with mom, dad and kids under one roof, is fading. In every state the numbers of unmarried couples, childless households and single-person households are growing faster than those comprised of married people with children."[9]

The Pew Research Center has conducted important examinations of the changes in family structure over time.[10] The center collected decades of research in a paper the title of which captures much of what has happened in America: "The Decline of Marriage and Rise of New Families."

The Pew researchers pointed out the dramatic nature of some of the changes found in the research data. "Social institutions that have been around for thousands of years generally change slowly, when they change at all," they noted. "But that's not the way things have been playing out with marriage and family since the middle of the twentieth century. Some scholars argue that in the past five decades, the basic architecture of these age-old institutions has changed as rapidly as at any time in human history."

The extent and speed of the change are important. If the changes were at the margins, or gradual, it might be hard to see a connection between these changes and broader economic trends and outcomes. But the swift and extensive changes mean it is more likely that we can see connections between these changes and ultimate economic outcomes.

So what has been happening?

GOING TO THE CHAPEL?

Let's start with marriage. Figure 2.1 gives a good sense of the steady change in marriage patterns over the last half century.

Of the total population, we see a smaller percentage of people who are married and increasing percentages of people who are divorced or who never married.

What's more, people who are getting married

FIGURE 2.1. CURRENT MARITAL STATUS, 1960–2008 (PERCENTAGE)

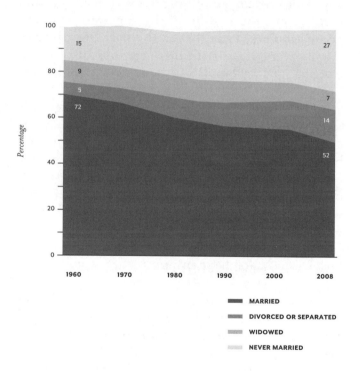

Note: Ages 18 and older. Numbers may not total to 100 percent due to rounding.

Source: Pew Social and Demographic Trends, "The Decline of Marriage and the Rise of New Families," Pew Research Center, November 18, 2010, http://www.pewsocialtrends. org/2010/11/18/the-decline-of-marriage-and-rise-of-new-families.

are doing so later today than in the past. For example, in 1960 almost 70 percent of adults ages 20 to 29 were married, while in the late 2000s about one quarter were hitched.[11]

Combine the rising age of marriage with another interesting social fact: increasing numbers of people are never getting married at all. Together the data suggest marriage is viewed differently today by Americans than it once was.

The policy analyst Ryan Streeter, examining data from the Population Reference Bureau, highlights some of the dramatic changes in marriage over time.[12] Consider table 2.1 from Streeter.

Streeter argues that a subtle but profound shift has occurred. "People just aren't aspiring to marriage as they used to, and by extension, they aren't aspiring to family as they used to, which reflects a huge shift in the moral understanding of the good life in America. Family—getting married, and then having kids—used to be woven together with other threads of the American Dream. Not so anymore."[13]

We are seeing more and more people who, in what might be termed their prime marriage and child-raising years, are opting against marriage altogether. Figure 2.2 is based on Census data and shows the declining percentages of people who are married between the ages of 35 and 44.

TABLE 2.1. PERCENTAGE OF PEOPLE WHO HAVE NEVER MARRIED BY SEX AND AGE, 1970, 2000, AND 2008

	1970	2000	2008
Women			
15–19	88	94	98
20–24	36	69	80
25–29	12	38	48
30–34	7	22	28
35 and older	7	8	10
Total	21	24	28
Men			
15–19	96	96	99
20–24	56	79	89
25–29	20	49	61
30–34	11	30	37
35 and older	7	11	13
Total	26	30	35

Source: Ryan Streeter, "Marriage Rates and the Libertarian-Libertine Assault on the American Dream," RyanStreeter.com, January 2, 2012, http://ryanstreeter. com/2012/01/02/marriage-rates-and-the-libertarian-libertine-assault-on-the-american-dream

FIGURE 2.2. PERCENTAGE OF PERSONS AGE 35–44 WHO WERE MARRIED, BY SEX, UNITED STATES

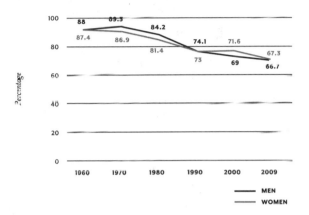

Source: State of Our Unions, "When Marriage Disappears," National Marriage Project at University of Virginia and Center for Marriage and Families at Institute for American Values, 2010.

With respect to marriage and family formation, the broad trends are clear. We also see big variations when we start to drill down and look at subsections of the American public.

For example, it turns out there are big class divisions when it comes to marriage today. "Marriage remains the norm for adults with a college education and good income," according to Pew. While 64 percent of Americans with a college degree were married, of those with a high school diploma or less, only 48 percent were married. This wasn't always the case. In the middle of the twentieth century, both the well educated and the less educated were just as likely to be married.[14]

These findings complement those of the American Enterprise Institute's Charles Murray in his best-selling book *Coming Apart*.[15] Murray found that the institution of marriage is still quite strong in affluent American precincts, but there has been

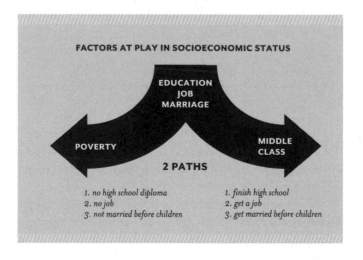

FACTORS AT PLAY IN SOCIOECONOMIC STATUS

EDUCATION
JOB
MARRIAGE

POVERTY

MIDDLE CLASS

2 PATHS

1. no high school diploma
2. no job
3. not married before children

1. finish high school
2. get a job
3. get married before children

tremendous erosion as one moves down the income and education scale.

While just 6 percent of children born to college-educated American mothers are born out of wedlock, the percentage for mothers with no more than a high school education is 44 percent.[16]

The University of Virginia's National Marriage Project, led by Brad Wilcox, has conducted some of the most significant academic research on the American family in recent years. Researchers there find "highly educated Americans, who make up 30 percent of the adult population, now enjoy marriages that are as stable and happy as those four decades ago." They point out that while for the last few decades "the retreat from marriage has been regarded largely as a problem afflicting the poor," that is no longer the case. "Today, it is spreading into the solid middle of the middle class."[17]

Part of what has happened is the decline of so-called shotgun marriages. The norm in the country used to be that if a girl became pregnant before she was married, the boyfriend would marry her. While there were exceptions to this, it was the case far more than not. Today shotgun marriages are a relic of the past.

The Nobel Prize–winning economist George Akerlof took stock of these changes in a famous paper called "Men without Children."[18] Akerlof noted that "in the old days a young man who got his girlfriend pregnant was expected to marry her; and she was expected to marry him." But he notes that:

> Since the early and mid-1960s marriage customs have changed dramatically. Perhaps they changed because of the technology shocks of the advent of female contraception and legalization of abortion— so that the guy did not have to marry the girl who became pregnant. Perhaps they changed for other reasons regarding, for example, the destigmatisation of out-of-wedlock birth, that grew out of the more temperate attitudes associated with the culture shocks of the 1960s. Perhaps the same secularization of society that allowed stores to be open on Sunday destigmatised out-of-wedlock birth so that the mothers felt free to keep their children. Whatever the reason for the change, the existence of that change is undeniable.[19]

The customs of Americans, their habits of heart and mind, have shifted dramatically when it comes to marriage.

DIVORCE

What about changes in family structure as related to divorce over time? Here it is important to be careful, because while the divorce rate can change, so, too, can the rate of marriage, so we need to account for that if we want to get an accurate overall picture.

Make no mistake, the divorce rate has risen significantly since World War II, with the biggest spike in divorce rates occurring in the 1970s. But it is important to note that divorce rates were unusually low in the 1950s and early 1960s, which makes the jump in divorce rates in the 1970s seem even more dramatic.

Divorce is one area where, from a Home Ec standpoint, there's some good news to report. Divorce rates peaked in the 1980s, at a rate of a little over five divorces per 1,000 people. Since then, the divorce rate has gradually declined, although it is still higher than it was at its low point of the early 1960s.

What about the explosion in divorce so many have talked about over the years? The spike in divorce rates seems most dramatic if you consider the rate not as a percentage of the total population but instead as the rate among married people. Here we see a truly dramatic increase in divorce in the 1970s and a gradual decline since then (see figure 2.3).

FIGURE 2.3. NUMBER OF DIVORCES PER 1,000 MARRIED WOMEN AGE 15 AND OLDER, BY YEAR, UNITED STATES [A]

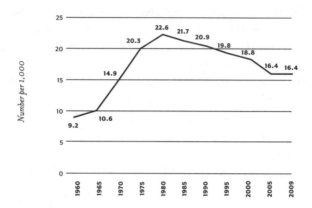

Source: State of Our Unions, "When Marriage Disappears," National Marriage Project at University of Virginia and Center for Marriage and Families at Institute for American Values, 2010.

The scholars Justin Wolfers and Betsey Stevenson have conducted fascinating research and analysis on family dynamics in recent years. They have pointed out that the number of children affected by divorce has changed over time.[20]

For example, in the 1950s, the average divorce involved 0.78 children while by 1968 that number had risen to 1.34. Since that time, however, fewer children have felt the effects of divorce. There are many reasons for this: family size is decreasing, for example, or divorce may be more concentrated among couples that never had children.

But one reason for the decreasing numbers of children affected by divorce—the most important from our Home Ec standpoint—is the increase in out-of-wedlock births.

OUT-OF-WEDLOCK BIRTHS: A NEW NORMAL

As dramatic as the changes in marriage and divorce have been, the most dramatic changes in family structure can be found when it comes to out-of-wedlock births. While only 5 percent of children were born out of wedlock in 1960, the percentage of births to unmarried women in 2010 was over 40 percent.[21]

As out-of-wedlock birth rates have risen, so have the rates of children raised by a single parent (typically the mother). While only 9 percent of children were raised by a single parent in 1960, over 25 percent were raised by a single parent in 2008.

Figure 2.4 illustrates the changes over five decades.

The *New York Times* reported in early 2012 that over half of births to women in the United States under the age of 30 are now out of wedlock.[22] As the

FIGURE 2.4. SHARE OF CHILDREN, BY NUMBER OF PARENTS IN HOUSEHOLD (PERCENTAGE)

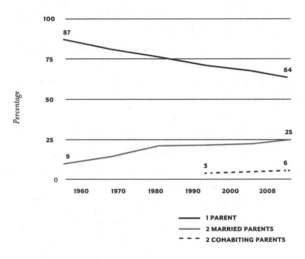

Note: Based on persons 17 and younger. Parents may be biological, adoptive, or stepparents. Children without any parent in the household are included in the base but not shown.

Source: Pew Social and Demographic Trends, "The Decline of Marriage and the Rise of New Families," Pew Research Center, November 18, 2010, http://www.pewsocialtrends.org/2010/11/18/the-decline-of-marriage-and-rise-of-new-families.

Times writers put it, "It used to be called illegitimacy. Now it is the new normal."

One can visualize this shift to a new normal

in the figure 2.5, from Brad Wilcox's National Marriage Project.[23]

Interestingly, according to the *Times*, "almost all of the rise in nonmarital births has occurred among couples living together."[24]

Sara McLanahan and her team of researchers at Princeton University-Brookings Institution Future of Children Project find that "more than 80 percent of unmarried parents are in a romantic relationship at the time of their child's birth, and most of these parents have high hopes for a future together."[25]

Indeed, despite increasingly delayed marriage and the rise in out-of-wedlock births, public opinion surveys still find strong rhetorical support among Americans for wanting to get married (even if it's after having kids as opposed to before).

Consider the following uniform agreement across social class about the importance of marriage (see figure 2.6).

Despite what Americans say about the importance of marriage, recent trends with respect to cohabiting couples with children do not inspire confidence. The odds of them remaining together for the long term are not encouraging.

"While in some countries such relationships endure at rates that resemble marriages," the *Times* reports, "in the United States they are more

FIGURE 2.5. PERCENTAGE OF BIRTHS TO NEVER-MARRIED WOMEN 15–44 YEARS OLD, BY EDUCATION AND YEAR

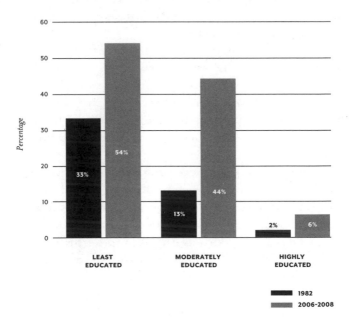

Note: Figures for 2006–08 include all nonmarried births, including the small number of women who were divorced or widowed at their child's birth.

Source: State of Our Unions, "When Marriage Disappears," National Marriage Project at University of Virginia and Center for Marriage and Families at Institute for American Values, 2010.

FIGURE 2.6. PERCENTAGE OF 25–60-YEAR-OLDS REPORTING MARRIAGE AS "VERY IMPORTANT" OR AS "ONE OF THE MOST IMPORTANT THINGS" TO THEM, BY EDUCATION LEVEL

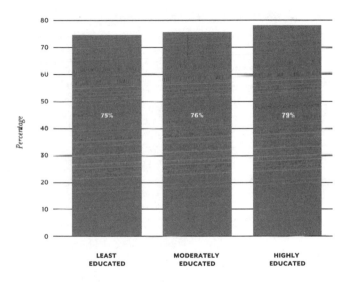

Source: State of Our Unions, "When Marriage Disappears," National Marriage Project at University of Virginia and Center for Marriage and Families at Institute for American Values, 2010.

FIGURE 2.7. PERCENTAGE OF CHILDREN UNDER AGE 18 LIVING WITH TWO MARRIED PARENTS, BY YEAR AND RACE, UNITED STATES

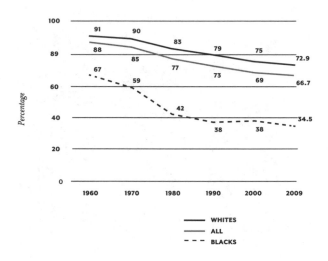

Source: State of Our Unions, "When Marriage Disappears," National Marriage Project at University of Virginia and Center for Marriage and Families at Institute for American Values, 2010.

than twice as likely to dissolve than marriages."[26] Researchers at the University of Michigan find that over 65 percent of cohabiting couples with kids are separated by the time the child turns ten years old.[27]

A higher percentage of kids born today is out-of-wedlock. Among those kids born to unmarried parents who were living together—and possibly providing a stable home environment—the large majority of their parents' relationships will fail.

Combine a divorce rate among married couples that is much higher than in the past with a rise in out-of-wedlock births and increasing numbers of parents who never marry at all, and over time America has, proportionally speaking, many fewer children living in intact, two-parent families.

WHAT IS DRIVING THE CHANGE?

What is driving some of the changes in family outlined here? There are many possible contributing factors.

For starters, greater acceptance of women in the workplace has meant women can earn an income to provide a measure of economic security to themselves and children outside the bonds of marriage.

Consider the change in the composition of the workforce in half a century outlined in figure 2.8.

As women rushed into the labor force in the 1960s, '70s, and '80s, their earning power increased. Scott Hankins and Mark Hoekstra found that positive income windfalls for women

FIGURE 2.8. DISTRIBUTION OF THE US LABOR FORCE BY GENDER, 1948–2009 (PERCENTAGE)

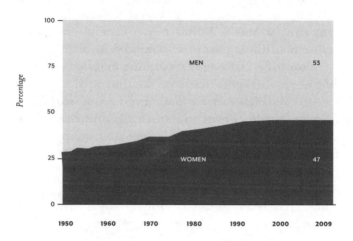

Note: Estimates reflect annual averages.

Source: Pew Social and Demographic Trends, "The Decline of Marriage and the Rise of New Families," Pew Research Center, November 18, 2010, http://www.pewsocialtrends. org/2010/11/18/the-decline-of-marriage-and-rise-of-new-families

make them less likely to marry.

"Results indicate that large income shocks significantly reduce the likelihood that single women marry. Specifically, we find that single women are six percentage points less likely to marry in the three years following the positive income shock, which represents a 40 percent decline. This suggests that additional income may remove some incentive for single women to marry, at least over the short-term."[28]

As women are able to earn good incomes and climb the income ladder, the economic "need" to get married diminishes.

Some believe changes in the global economy that have yielded a decline in middle-class manufacturing jobs in the United States have driven middle-class males from the labor force, making them less marriageable. The decline of labor unions is also fingered as a culprit in this dynamic.

Perhaps there is something to this (see figure 2.9). As the researchers at the University of Virginia's National Marriage Project note, "in today's information economy, the manual skills of moderately educated Americans are now markedly less valued than the intellectual and social skills of the highly educated .... By contrast, highly educated Americans, including men, have seen their real wages increase since the 1970s and have not experienced marked increases in unemployment (except during the Great Recession, but over the last two years, unemployment has been much worse for moderately educated men)."[29]

FIGURE 2.9. PERCENTAGE OF 25–60-YEAR-OLD MEN UNEMPLOYED AT SOME POINT OVER THE LAST TEN YEARS, BY EDUCATION LEVEL AND DECADE

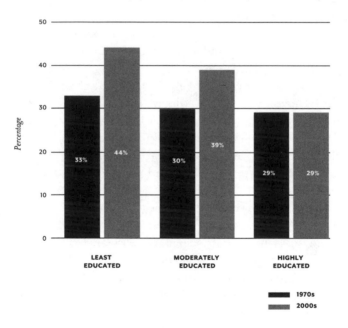

Source: State of Our Unions, "When Marriage Disappears," National Marriage Project at University of Virginia and Center for Marriage and Families at Institute for American Values, 2010.

This explanation only gets us so far. We would be prudent not to overstate the effect. As Charles Murray has explained, changes in the economy cannot explain all or even most of what has happened in the last half century. "If changes in the availability of well-paying jobs determined dropout rates over the entire half-century from 1960 to 2010, we should have seen a reduction in dropouts during that long stretch of good years. But instead we saw an increase, from 8.9% of white males ages 30 to 49 in 1994 to 11.9% as of March 2008, before the financial meltdown."[30]

In other words, purely economic explanations for the changes in marriage and birth patterns will get us only a little way in the face of the dramatic scope of the changes that have occurred.

Other changes influencing the shape of family life include shifting attitudes about the acceptability of having sex outside of marriage. Many fewer people think it is wrong to have sex outside marriage, which means many fewer people need to get married if they want to have sex. Easy accessibility to pregnancy control technologies and legal abortion are also playing a role (see figure 2.10).

One of the more surprising changes in these attitudes over time can be found among highly educated Americans. Despite—or perhaps because

FIGURE 2.10. PERCENTAGE OF 25–60-YEAR-OLDS BELIEVING PREMARITAL SEX IS ALWAYS WRONG, BY EDUCATION LEVEL AND DECADE

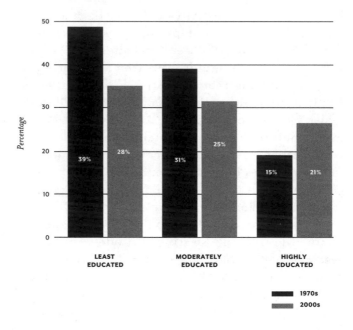

Source: State of Our Unions, "When Marriage Disappears," National Marriage Project at University of Virginia and Center for Marriage and Families at Institute for American Values, 2010.

of—the greater culture-wide acceptance of premarital sex, Americans with high educational attainment are now more likely to think it is wrong today than they did in the 1970s.

There has also been a decline in religious participation over the last several decades (see figure 2.11), even if the United States remains far more religious than comparable developed countries.

Organized religions place a heavy emphasis on the importance and sanctity of marriage and family life, and the decline of religiosity has likely corresponded to a weakening in the family.[31] Surely another factor influencing trends in marriage, sex, and out-of-wedlock births is the rise of what Mark Bauerlein has called "the separate lives of adolescence."[32] Building on the influential work of social scientist James Coleman and his landmark work *The Adolescent Society*,[33] Bauerlein recently examined the lives, attitudes, and habits of American adolescents. He finds they live in a subculture of their own making, connected by technology and largely outside the sustained influence of adult prerogatives and preferences.

As a result, he says, they "take longer to mature, to outgrow the values of adolescence. They acquire adult attitudes in their twenties, not in their late teens. Whether they emerge at age thirty as

FIGURE 2.11. RELIGIOUS ATTENDANCE

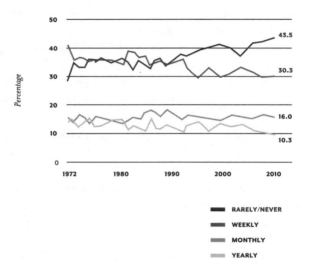

Notes: Figures are biannual 1972–90, individual years in 1991 and 1993, and biennial 1994–2010. "Rarely/ never" attend religious services 0–1 times per year. "Yearly" attend several times a year. "Monthly" attend 1–3 times a month. "Weekly" attend about every week, or one or more times a week.

Source: "Church Attendance Is Declining," The Heritage Foundation, familyfacts.org, n.d., http://www.familyfacts.org/charts/620/church-attendance-is-declining.

responsible and virtuous as they would have remains to be seen."[34] Either way it is hardly surprising, given this dynamic, that for many, marriage and child rearing are coming later and later if at all.

Whatever the reasons, the complex interplay of ideas and morality, technology, norms, culture, habits, attitudes, and economic forces has had a profound effect on family structure. These changes in family structure have had profound economic consequences for individuals. We turn to these consequences in the next chapter.

3

THE ECONOMIC CONSEQUENCES OF CHANGING FAMILY STRUCTURE

"There are some massive externalities to the behavior of other people."

—Jason Collins[35]

What if the decline of marriage and the rise of out-of-wedlock births and other changes to family structure had no broader economic consequences for individuals? What if they even had positive consequences? Surely this would inform how we think about these changes.

After all, there are many examples of children who grew up with a single parent but went on to be successful and live normal, happy lives. Or women who flourished after leaving abusive and unloving husbands.

Dysfunction in the home is not destiny. Presidents Ronald Reagan, Bill Clinton, and Barack Obama, for example, all grew up in dysfunctional home environments. Despite—or perhaps because of—their upbringing, they were extraordinarily high achievers.

At the same time, we all know people who grew up with all of life's advantages—a stable family, wealth, a good education—and yet developed serious problems or never amounted to much.

Whatever anecdotes we may find, broader trends show that most of the consequences of unstable home life are negative.

Let's start with some of the most dramatic pieces of data on the economic importance of intact families. Ron Haskins and Isabel Sawhill are two scholars at the Brookings Institution and some of the country's leading thinkers on urban problems, welfare, income inequality, and social mobility.

In a review of Census Bureau data, they found that "if young people finish high school, get a job, and get married before they have children, they have about a 2 percent chance of falling into poverty and nearly a 75 percent chance of joining the middle class by earning $50,000 or more per year."[36]

If you think about it for a moment, that is not an impossibly high bar. Finish high school (not even college). Work. Don't have a baby before you are married. If you do these three things, the odds you will be poor are tiny.

Sara McLanahan and Gary Sandefur put the matter bluntly in their book, *Growing Up with a Single Parent*:

> Children who grow up in a household with only one biological parent are worse off, on average, than children who grow up in a household with both of their biological parents, regardless of the parents' race or educational background, regardless of

whether the parents are married when the child is born, and regardless of whether the resident parent remarries.[37]

They go on to add,

adolescents who have lived apart from one of their parents during some period of childhood are twice as likely to drop out of high school, twice as likely to have a child before age twenty, and one and a half times as likely to be "idle"—out of school and out of work—in their late teens and early twenties.[38]

McLanahan and Sandefur are careful researchers and point out that "growing up with a single parent is just one of many factors that put children at risk of failure." But there is little doubt that the economic problems created by single motherhood are sizable.

As social scientists David Ellwood and Christopher Jencks put it,

From an economic perspective, the most troubling feature of family change has been the spread of single motherhood. Single mothers seldom command high wages. They also find it unusually difficult to work long hours, since they must also care for their children. Many get very little in child support from the absent father, and even generous child support payments provide less support than a resident father with the same income would normally provide. While poor single mothers are eligible for various forms of public assistance, neither legislators nor voters have wanted to make such assistance at all generous, lest generosity encourage still more women to raise children on their own. *The spread of single-mother families has therefore played a major role in the persistence of poverty* (emphasis added).[39]

It is important to spend some time thinking about why the outcomes for those raised by a single mother, of those raised in what McLanahan has called "fragile families," would be so much worse.[40]

HUMAN AND SOCIAL CAPITAL

Part of the greater risk for these children can be traced to what Nobel Prize–winning economist Gary Becker called "human capital" and what social scientist James Coleman called "social capital."

What do we mean when we talk about human or social capital? The traditional notion of capital brings to mind a physical object that could be used to generate income: a piece of construction equipment, a factory, a farm, a building, a railroad, a computer network, and on and on. This is tangible stuff we can see and touch.

Human capital is the knowledge, education, habits, willpower—all the internal stuff that is largely intangible—a person has that helps produce an income.

People are born with certain amounts of human capital from which they cannot be separated. They have inborn intellectual talents and capacities, for example. But people can also accumulate lots of additional human capital over time. Much crucial human capital is developed when people are young and throughout their adolescence.

It is worth noting that human capital is much more important in an economic sense than many people appreciate at first glance (and part of why we focus on it in the context of Home Ec). For example, a research paper from the Bureau of Economic Analysis estimated the total stock of physical capital and human capital in the United States. The physical capital is all the factories, equipment, and so on that helps companies generate incomes. The human capital is all the knowledge, talent, and internal capacities that help a person make a living.

Based on the future income streams Americans could generate, the value today of all the human capital in America is over $700 trillion.[41] This is much greater than the value of physical capital, worth an estimated $45 trillion (see figure 3.1).

What do we mean by "social capital"? McLanahan and Sandefur describe social capital as "an asset

FIGURE 3.1. HUMAN AND PHYSICAL CAPITAL STOCK, UNITED STATES (TRILLIONS OF DOLLARS)

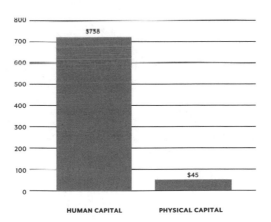

Source: Michael S. Christian, "Human Capital Accounting in the United States: Context, Measurement, and Application" (working paper, Wisconsin Center for Education Research, July 2011), http://www.bea.gov/papers/pdf/human_capital_accounting_in_the_united_states.pdf.

that is created and maintained by relationships of commitment and trust. It functions as a conduit of information as well as a source of emotional and economic support, and *it can be just as important as financial capital in promoting children's future success*" (emphasis added).[42]

Human and social capital reinforce and complement each other. Human capital helps people develop their social capital, which in turn helps them further develop their human capital.

The family is among the most important institutions for developing human and social capital. The social critic Christopher Lasch vividly describes how the family functions as a generator of valuable capital. "As the chief agency of socialization," Lasch writes,

> the family reproduces cultural patterns in the individual. It not only imparts ethical norms, providing the child with his first instruction in the prevailing social rules, it profoundly shapes his character, in ways of which he is not even aware. The family instills modes of thought and action that become habitual. Because of its enormous emotional influence, it colors all of a child's subsequent experience.[43]

Lasch was one of the most penetrating analysts of the subtle ways families shape individuals. While he did not speak explicitly in terms of human and social capital, he is worth quoting at length for his powerful insights into the ways family develops and sculpts important determinants of economic success and human flourishing. "The union of love and discipline in the same persons, mother and father, creates a highly charged environment in which the child learns lessons he will never get over," Lasch claims.

> These lessons are not necessarily the explicit lessons his parents wish him to master. He develops an unconscious predisposition to act in certain ways and to recreate in later life, in his relations with lovers and authorities, his earliest experiences. Parents first embody love and power, and each of their actions conveys to the child, quite independently of their overt intentions, the injunctions and constraints by means of which society attempts to organize experience. If the reproduction of culture were simply a matter of formal instruction and discipline, it could be left to the schools. But it also requires that culture be embedded in personality.

> Socialization makes the individual want to do what he has to do; the family is the agency to which society entrusts this complex and delicate task.[44]

Given the family's importance, Lasch argues, "changes in its size and structure, in its emotional organization, and in its relations with the outside world must have enormous impact on the development of personality. *Changes in character structure, in turn, accompany or underlie changes in economic and political life*" (emphasis added).[45]

Human and social capital—including a person's character, which is shaped by the family—constitutes a crucial part of the skill set a person uses to get a job, start a career, and succeed in the economy.

THE IMPORTANCE OF NONCOGNITIVE SKILLS

Every person is equipped with varying amounts of cognitive skills: IQ, innate faculties, and accumulated learning from schooling and other sources of knowledge. Every person also has important noncognitive skills. Nobel Prize–winning economist James Heckman has spent many years studying the importance to economic success of skills, including noncognitive skills.

Heckman notes that "modern society is based on skills, and inequality in achievement across all race and ethnic groups is primarily due to inequality in skills. Both cognitive and personality skills determine life success."[46]

This emphasis on both cognitive and noncognitive (or personality) skills is difficult to overstate. The importance of cognitive skills is obvious; these skills include the ability to read and write well or to solve math and logic problems. A person will need these skills to perform well in just about any job.

Developing these cognitive skills helps develop the capacity for reason and analytical thinking that helps one's economic prospects down the road. This is part of the reason policymakers put such a heavy emphasis on the importance of a good education.

What about the noncognitive skills? As it turns out, these are also critical for success in life, including economic success. These include the ability to play fairly with others, to delay gratification, to control emotions, to develop and maintain networks of friends and acquaintances, and much more.

These noncognitive skills are an important part of overall human and social capital. For starters, these skills help one develop full cognitive capacities—the ability to stay in school and graduate, for example. They also help as tools for success in navigating the modern world.

Many jobs in a modern economy rely heavily on noncognitive social skills. Indeed, the service sector is growing rapidly relative to other sectors in the economy, such as farming and manufacturing. As the economy evolves, human and social capital play an increasingly important role in the ability to gain and maintain employment.

What does the home environment have to do with all this? "Families are major producers of skills," Heckman says.

> They do much more than pass along their genes. *Inequality in skills and schools is strongly linked to inequality in family environments.* While the exact mechanisms through which families produce skills are actively being investigated, a lot is already known. Parenting matters. *The true measure of child poverty and advantage is the quality of parenting a child receives,* not just the money available to the household (emphasis added).[47]

Heckman explains the complex nature of skill formation and development and the role that family structure plays in it. "Life cycle skill formation is dynamic in nature," he writes. "Skill begets skill; motivation begets motivation. Motivation cross-fosters skill, and skill cross-fosters motivation. *If a child is not motivated to learn and engage early on in life, the more likely it is that when the child becomes an adult, he or she will fail in social and economic life*" (emphasis added).[48]

It is increasingly clear that some noncognitive skills, such as self-control, are not entirely genetic, inborn, or innate. They can be improved and enhanced over time, and the home environment plays a role in shaping and developing those skills.

In their book *Willpower*, the cognitive psychologist Roy Baumeister and science writer John Tierney note an interesting finding relevant to this discussion. The writers describe psychology tests administered to children in which they earn a delayed reward if they exhibit a strong degree of self-control. The children were presented with a choice of candy bars. One candy bar was very large and cost ten times as much as a smaller candy bar. If the children wanted the larger and more valuable reward, however, they had to wait ten days before they could receive it. If they chose the smaller candy bar, they could have it right away. "Children who had a father in the home were far more willing than others to choose the delayed reward,"[49] they write. While there is little doubt that genes play a role in a child's self-control, several studies that control for genetics still show a difference.[50]

ECONOMIC MOBILITY

Family structure also influences economic mobility—the ability to move up the rungs of the economic ladder during working years.

Thomas DeLeire and Leonard Lopoo of the Economic Mobility Project analyzed a data set that tracked the economic performance of parents and children from the late 1960s. Since children from wealthier homes have obvious economic and social advantages over those from poorer households, the researchers controlled for that and put together "the first study . . . that examines how family structure is associated with the income of children when they reach adulthood, separating out the potential influence of parental income."[51]

They found that "it is not true that parents' income alone enables children to succeed."[52] A more detailed look reveals a more nuanced picture.

> Characteristics of families, including such diverse factors as parenting style, parental aspirations, and the neighborhoods in which families live, contribute to the formation of children's human capital. In particular, *the structure of the family in which a child grows up could have as large an impact as income, or larger, on subsequent economic outcomes* (emphasis added).[53]

They found that "family structure influences the economic mobility of children. Divorce is particularly harmful for children's mobility." For example, "among children who start in the bottom third of the income distribution, only 26 percent with divorced parents move up to the middle or top third as adults, compared to 42 percent of children born to unmarried mothers and 50 percent of children with continuously married parents."[54]

It is not just children who benefit economically from a stable and healthy family environment. Pew researchers found that "as the country shifts away from marriage, a smaller proportion of adults are experiencing the economic gains that typically accrue from marriage."[55]

The Pew researchers compared the median household incomes of married adults with unmarried adults in 1960 and again in 2008. Half a century ago, the gap in household incomes was 12 percent. In 2008, the gap had grown to over 40 percent.

"The widening of the gap is explained," the report says,

> partly by the increased share of wives in the workforce (61% in 2008, versus 32% in 1960) and partly by the increased differential in the educational attainment of the married and the unmarried.
>
> The net result is that a marriage gap and a socio-economic gap have been growing

side by side for the past half century, and each may be feeding off the other.[56]

The marriage gap coincides with differential poverty rates. Research from Columbia University's National Center for Children in Poverty found that only 5 percent of married-family households were poor at some point within a given year, compared with almost 30 percent of single-parent households.[57]

THE FAMILY AND THE POOR

The accumulation of evidence about the economic harm resulting from changing family structure is beginning to persuade skeptics. For example, Nicholas Kristof of the *New York Times*, who has spent years investigating the lives and material conditions of poor people around the world, writes, "Liberals sometimes feel that it is narrow-minded to favor traditional marriage. Over time, my reporting on poverty has led me to disagree: Solid marriages have a huge beneficial impact on the lives of the poor (more so than in the lives of the middle class, who have more cushion when things go wrong)."[58]

Consider Kristof's comment in the context of debates about, say, rising income inequality or rising wealth disparities. While global income inequality has been shrinking, there is some evidence that income inequality had been increasing in the United

States (not accounting for government transfers). Those at the top of the economic ladder were doing well while those closer to the bottom were stagnating or falling behind, their dependence on government growing.

Americans worry about these disparities because we share a concern for the poor and the least advantaged. Yet, as key as it is, we rarely include the family structure in discussions of alleviating income inequality or helping the poor.

The accumulation of evidence is showing that changes in family structure are a big part of this overall story. If we want to talk constructively about issues such as poverty or income inequality, we need to bring what has happened to the family into the picture.

As we'll see in the next chapter, perhaps we shouldn't be surprised that Home Ec has been left out of the broader discussion. There was a moment when both liberals and conservatives sought to bring this issue to the center of the American conversation, but, for a host of reasons, that moment was lost.

4

THE LONG SHADOW OF
THE MOYNIHAN REPORT

"The fundamental problem . . . is that of family structure."

—Daniel Patrick Moynihan, 1965[59]

Daniel Patrick Moynihan had one of the most fascinating and full careers of any American public figure in the twentieth century. He was a US senator from New York for twenty-four years. He was an accomplished diplomat, serving as US ambassador to India and then to the United Nations in the mid-1970s. He served in four different presidential administrations, for both Democrats and Republicans, from John F. Kennedy to Gerald R. Ford.

He was also one of the most interesting thinkers in the history of American governance. Moynihan's work as a social scientist and intellectual is what is most important to Home Ec.

Part of Moynihan's worldview was shaped by having grown up in New York City. His family frequently moved around throughout the city and the suburbs. Moynihan knew periods of relative prosperity, but growing up in Depression-era America, he also knew long periods of economic insecurity. When Moynihan was young, his father abandoned the family and moved to the West Coast. Moynihan never saw him again.

James Patterson, the author of a marvelous book about Moynihan, remarked that

> though it is never easy to draw a straight line connecting youthful experiences to later beliefs, it is possible that the trials of Pat's early years heightened his sense of vulnerability. The wrenching times he experienced in New York may also have made him prone to worry that something apocalyptic would render the nation incapable of getting through crises.[60]

Moynihan was a gifted thinker and writer. After graduating from high school in New York, he went to Tufts University in Boston and later to the London School of Economics. He also did a stint in the US military.

A committed political liberal, Moynihan believed government policymakers, armed with findings from the social sciences, could be a force for good, advancing policies and programs to help the poor and disadvantaged.

In the 1950s, he gravitated to political and intellectual circles in New York, where he began to make a name for himself as a writer and analyst with a first-rate mind. Moynihan moved to Washington in 1961 to work in the Kennedy administration's Department of Labor.

Moynihan stayed on at the Department of Labor into the presidency of Lyndon Johnson and pursued work on poverty, employment, education, and crime. He became keenly interested in the plight of urban blacks and used the tools at his disposal to analyze the problems of the metropolitan poor.

Riots in Harlem and other urban centers in 1964 brought new attention to the problems of our country's inner cities. These issues—poverty, unemployment, illegitimacy, crime, and more— would come to consume Moynihan, then an assistant secretary of labor.

Moynihan eventually produced a paper analyzing the problems of American inner-city black life. *The Negro Family: The Case for National Action* was later dubbed *The Moynihan Report*.[61] The report brought a once obscure academic and wonk to national renown.

Moynihan noted in the paper that while American blacks had made considerable political progress in recent years—including the passage of the landmark Civil Rights Act—the material situation of American blacks, particularly urban blacks, was getting worse.

One troubling sign was a seemingly incongruous social trend Moynihan identified. While rates of unemployment were dropping in the 1960s, welfare rates were increasing. Most social scientists would have predicted the opposite: as more workers find jobs, the need for welfare should decline.

As the scholar Kay Hymowitz put it, "In the past, policymakers had assumed that if the male heads of household had jobs, women and children would be provided for. This no longer seemed true. Even while more black men . . . were getting jobs, more black women were joining the welfare rolls."[62]

This crisscrossing trend—rising welfare dependence coincident with lowering unemployment—came to be called "Moynihan's scissors."

Surely something puzzling was happening in American cities. What was driving these developments? There there were several factors, but change in family structure was central to the decline of the material condition of the urban poor.

"The evidence—not final, but powerfully persuasive—is that the Negro family in the urban ghettos is crumbling," Moynihan writes. "A middle class group has managed to save itself, but for vast numbers of the unskilled, poorly educated city working class the fabric of conventional social relationships has all but disintegrated. There are indications that the situation may have been arrested in the past few years, but the general post war trend is unmistakable. So long as this situation persists, the cycle of poverty and disadvantage will continue to repeat itself."[63]

Reading the *Moynihan Report* almost a half century after its publication is arresting on many levels.

The most obvious is the use of terminology and expressions now long abandoned—"Negro" chief among them.

Another arresting element of the report is how much a report written about the "Negro" family of the 1960s could be repurposed to describe the state of Hispanic and white families today.

"At the heart of the deterioration of Negro society," Moynihan wrote, "is the deterioration of the Negro family." What specific deterioration did Moynihan have in mind?

- "Nearly a quarter of Negro women living in cities who have ever married are divorced, separated, or are living apart from their husbands."
- "Both white and Negro illegitimacy rates have been increasing, although from dramatically different bases. The white rate was 2 percent in 1940; it was 3.07 percent in 1963. In that period, the Negro rate went from 16.8 percent to 23.6 percent."
- "As a direct result of this high rate of divorce, separation, and desertion, a very large percent of Negro families are headed by females. While the percentage of such families among whites has been dropping since 1940, it has been rising among Negroes."
- "The percent of nonwhite families headed by a female is more than double the percent for

whites. Fatherless nonwhite families increased by a sixth between 1950 and 1960, but held constant for white families."

· "It has been estimated that only a minority of Negro children reach the age of 18 having lived all their lives with both of their parents."[64]

Moynihan went on at length to discuss some of the roots of the dynamic affecting black life in America: the legacy of slavery, reconstruction, the effects of urbanization, low education levels, and more. He discussed what he called the "tangle of pathology" harming urban black communities: crime, out-of-wedlock births, divorce, drug use, and alcoholism.

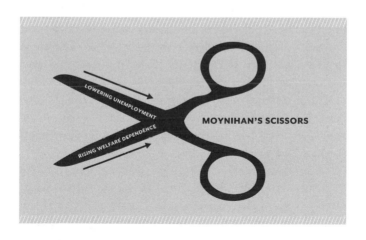

The report generated a firestorm of controversy, especially after the Watts riots in late summer 1965. Many critics of the report failed to appreciate the nuance, care, and humanity at the report's core. Moynihan was eventually accused by some of blaming the victim. The critics said Moynihan was aiming to divert responsibility for bad behavior. But Moynihan had done no such thing. He wrote with great compassion and concern for the urban poor.

Given the enduring and persistent harms of an evil slave system, Jim Crow, and other assaults on American blacks, "that the Negro American has survived at all is extraordinary," Moynihan wrote. "A lesser people might simply have died out, as indeed others have. That the Negro community has not only survived, but in this political generation has entered national affairs as a moderate, humane, and constructive national force is the highest testament to the healing powers of the democratic ideal and the creative vitality of the Negro people.

"But it may not be supposed that the Negro American community has not paid a fearful price for the incredible mistreatment to which it has been subjected over the past three centuries."[65]

Historian Steven F. Hayward points out that the *Moynihan Report* was swept into two powerful political currents gathering force in American politics at the time: feminism and the civil rights struggle.[66] Many feminists were reluctant to embrace the idea that a rise of single-mother households was a problem for society, and some in the civil rights movement perceived Moynihan's emphasis on problems in black family life as wrong-headed.

Hayward writes in his book *The Age of Reagan* about a White House conference on the family convened during the Johnson administration after the release of the *Moynihan Report*.[67] The conference "turned into a vehicle for the radical rejection of Moynihan along with the rejection of traditional understandings of the family." Hayward writes:

> Soon critics began asking: What's wrong with single-parent families anyway? Andrew Young, whom Martin Luther King tapped as his representative to the White House conference on the issue, said that 'there probably isn't anything wrong with the Negro family as it exists.' The concern with family stability, critics said in a now-familiar refrain, was an attempt to 'impose middle class values' on the poor. In fact, it was asserted, the black female headed household is 'a cultural pattern superior in its vitality to middle-class mores.'
>
> At the opening of the planning session [for the conference], White House conference

director Beryl Bernhard attempted to soothe the critics by announcing that 'I want you to know that I have been reliably informed that no such person as Daniel Patrick Moynihan exists.' But the critics were not to be appeased. A planning panel reported out the sense of the delegates that 'All families should have the right to evolve in directions of their own choosing . . . and should have the supports—economic and non-economic—to exercise that right.' The conference planners demanded that 'the question of "family stability" be stricken entirely from that agenda.' The White House—and liberals—beat a hasty retreat; it would be 20 years before the subject of black family stability could be discussed again.[68]

FROM THE NEGRO FAMILY TO ALL FAMILIES

The *Moynihan Report* is worth revisiting today in the context of the longer-term trends that have occurred over the last half century, not just in black communities but in the rest of America.

For example, when Moynihan claimed there was a crisis in the black family, the illegitimacy rate among American blacks was a little over 23 percent. This alarming statistic was at the heart of his call for national action.

FIGURE 4.1. SHARE OF BIRTHS TO UNMARRIED WOMEN BY RACE AND ETHNICITY (PERCENTAGE)

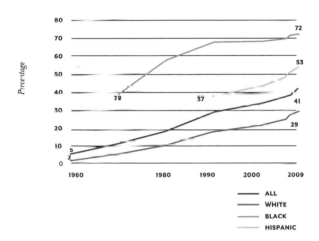

Note: 2008 data are preliminary. Hispanics are of any race. Whites and blacks include only non-Hispanics.

Source: Pew Social and Demographic Trends, "The Decline of Marriage and the Rise of New Families," Pew Research Center, November 18, 2010, http://www.pewsocialtrends. org/2010/11/18/the-decline-of-marriage-and-rise-of-new-families.

Fast-forward to today.

As figure 4.1 shows, the illegitimacy rate for white Americans is 29 percent, significantly higher than the alarming rate Moynihan documented. The rate for the whole country is over 40 percent. If trends continue, the illegitimacy rate for the country will be more than double what the black rate was when Moynihan issued his call to action.

Why did the deteriorating state of the black family matter so much to Moynihan? He writes:

> The role of the family in shaping character and ability is so pervasive as to be easily overlooked. The family is the basic social unit of American life; it is the basic socializing unit. By and large, adult conduct in society is learned as a child. A fundamental insight of psychoanalytic theory, for example, is that the child learns a way of looking at life in his early years through which all later experience is viewed and which profoundly shapes his adult conduct.[69]

Moynihan was rightly worried that the erosion of this character-forming institution would have baleful economic and social consequences for American blacks. But many of the things happening in black American families in the 1960s that worried Moynihan have since happened in other groups as well.

PROGRESS IS SELDOM A FREE LUNCH

In 2002 an academic conference was held at Syracuse University to discuss the state of family life around the world. Moynihan was invited to give a keynote lecture. Patterson's excellent book *Freedom Is Not Enough* recalls the conference.[70]

Many of the conferees noted that the changes Moynihan documented in 1965 were now widespread across the developed world. Marriage was in decline, out-of-wedlock births were on the rise. These changes yielded different outcomes, depending on the country.

For example, cohabitation was on the rise in northern Europe as in the United States. But while Scandinavian countries had much higher rates of out-of-wedlock births than the United States, they had far higher percentages of unmarried parents staying together to raise their children.

When the conferees discussed the reasons for the rise in out-of-wedlock births, they focused on many of the culprits discussed earlier. Some fingered poverty and loss of employment opportunities due to changes in the economy. Others pointed to changing norms and attitudes with respect to marriage and family formation. Still others pointed to the decline in religious participation or deteriorating economic and social conditions in communities.

The social scientist Christopher Jencks argues

"the biggest factor was more widespread cultural acceptance of two ideals: 'tolerance' and 'personal freedom.' These ideals made most Americans and Western Europeans less willing to treat sex, childbearing, and marriage as matters of right and wrong."

Jencks went on to say, "I think that was probably progress, though I sometimes have my doubts. Still, progress is seldom a free lunch."[71]

THE UNIMAGINABLE HAPPENED

Moynihan's remarkable political career had him involved not only in welfare and social policy but also in intelligence, foreign affairs, diplomacy, city politics, and much more. He witnessed—and was an important figure in—an extraordinary array of world-changing events, from the civil rights achievements, to the opening with China, to the collapse of the Soviet Union, to the renaissance of urban life in his beloved New York City, to the emergence of the United States as the world's sole superpower.

But as the Ethics and Public Policy Center's Peter Wehner notes, when Moynihan was asked what he believed to be the biggest change he had witnessed over the long arc of his career, he said, "The biggest change, in my judgment, is that the family structure has come apart all over the North Atlantic world."

This was a change that happened "in an historical instant. Something that was not imaginable 40 years ago has happened."[72]

It is possible to imagine that the reaction to the *Moynihan Report* could have gone differently, that it could have put rapidly changing family structure at the center of the American discussion over economic success and well-being. Instead the report became caught up in the country's bitter politics. Many of the issues his report highlighted—a decline in marriage, rising illegitimacy rates, and so on—moved into the country's emerging culture-war politics.

As a result, the structure of the family—its importance in forming valuable human and social capital, in forming character—has not been as central to discussions of economic outcomes as it should. The long shadow of the *Moynihan Report* still looms over American life.

Next, we will examine what we should do about the trends and problems first highlighted by Moynihan in the context of black America but now gathering steam among almost all segments of American life.

5

WHAT TO DO AND THE LIMITS OF POLICY

"Practically every example of [a book aspiring to analyze a social or political problem], no matter how shrewd or rich its survey of the question at hand, finishes with an obligatory prescription that is utopian, banal, unhelpful, or out of tune with the rest of the book."

—David Greenberg[73]

"For those who want to alter family structure, we can only offer one bit of advice: treat anyone who claims to know how to do this with a high degree of skepticism."

—David Ellwood and Christopher Jencks[74]

This is the point in a book where an author typically devotes a chapter to answering the question, "okay, what do we do now?" In other words, if we take it as given that many of the changes in American family life over the last half century have had harmful economic consequences, what can be done to make things better?

Unlike most chapters of this kind, this one will not propose a laundry list of fixes. The writer George Will explains the reason.

In a speech at the American Enterprise Institute in honor of James Q. Wilson, perhaps America's greatest social scientist of the twentieth century, Will remarked that social science was important "not because social science is supposed to teach us what to do, but because social sciences instead teach us what is not working."[75]

The social science research of the last half century has helped us understand changes in marriage, childbearing, attitudes about the family, and more. While there is still much to discover, such research has helped us document the radical and sudden transformations of the American family. We have learned that the way the family has evolved over the course of fifty years has yielded an array of problems and suboptimal outcomes for a great many people.

The family—once described by former Secretary of Education William Bennett as the "original and best Department of Health, Education, and Welfare"[76]—is for many Americans no longer working as well as it should in terms of equipping its members with the human and social capital, stability, skills, and character formation they need to thrive.

Despite policymakers' and politicians' frequent invocation of social science findings to push for all manner of political changes, social science is not a good instrument for telling us, as Will put it, "what to do."

INTERVENTIONS

That said, it is in our nature to want to fix a problem when we see it. When faced with the broader societal consequences of family breakdown, the push for solutions is inescapable in a democracy. With that in mind, what are some approaches to the problems resulting from family breakdown?

One approach is to forget altogether doing much to reverse the transformation of the family. Instead, we should focus our efforts on alleviating specific harms that arise in part from family breakdown.

This is the approach taken by scholars such as Nobel Prize–winning economist James Heckman, among many others. Heckman has long been an advocate of large state interventions aimed at helping at-risk children. Specifically, he advocates "large investments in early childhood education from birth to age five."[77] In this way, the state assumes many of the responsibilities that in an earlier time would have been reserved for parents, communities, and family members.

Massive early childhood interventions hold some hope of helping equip at-risk kids with some of the soft capital they need to succeed. Heckman argues, "Smart, high-quality, and targeted early childhood development promotes health, economic, and social outcomes by fusing cognitive skills with the critical social skills of attentiveness, persistence, and sociability."[78]

What kinds of interventions are we talking about? One influential study involves the HighScope Perry Preschool project, a quality, two-year nursery program for poor black children living in Ypsilanti, Michigan. Researchers have followed the children who participated in the program for over half a century.

What did the researchers find? Heckman says,

Children in the program were less likely to commit crimes, less likely to drop out of school, and more likely to be productive, perseverant, socially engaged citizens with higher wages. As the years pass, the data reveal less teen pregnancy for girls, reduced absenteeism for boys, and less need for special or remedial education. A lot of other research bolsters these conclusions, along with growing neuro-scientific evidence of the impact of early learning on the brain.[79]

Writing in *The New Republic*, Jonathan Cohn reports on several studies on interventions in the first two years of a child's life that show considerable promise in reducing problems down the road. Cohn writes:

a scientific revolution that has taken place in the last decade or so illuminates a different way to address the dysfunctions associated with childhood hardship. This science suggests that many of these problems have roots earlier than is commonly understood—especially during the first two years of life. Researchers . . . have shown how adversity during this period affects the brain, down to the level of DNA—establishing for the first time a causal connection between trouble in very early childhood and later in life. And they have also shown a way to prevent some of these problems—if action is taken during those crucial first two years. [80]

That the interventions happen early in life is a key to their success. Heckman points out that there is very little evidence that interventions later in life—when someone is already in, say, middle school or high school or an adult—can do much to empower people with the character traits and skills they need to flourish.

He also points out that much of the money spent on the remedial efforts later in life is wasted and would be better spent on significant targeted interventions when children are younger, at preschool age and earlier. "Many of our social problems, such as crime, are traced to an absence of the social and emotional skills, such as perseverance and self-control, that can be fostered by early learning," he says. Furthermore, "crime costs taxpayers an estimated $1 trillion per year."[81]

It is difficult not to be excited about this and similar research looking at early childhood interventions. The problems these programs are trying to address in terms of family dysfunction and disarray are so great, and the harmful economic and social consequences of family inequality so pronounced, that anything that might help is worth study and analysis.

As James Q. Wilson has pointed out, "hardly a state in the Union has not been affected by the discovery in Ypsilanti, Michigan, that twelve hours a week of preschool experience for underprivileged three- and four-year olds increases the proportion of them completing school and reduces the proportion reporting . . . that they had engaged in serious misconduct."[82]

While it almost certainly makes sense to experiment with shifting scarce resources away from ineffective, later-stage interventions to higher potential, early interventions, we should be skeptical about what can ultimately be achieved. While there is evidence that early-stage intervention programs yield positive results, we should not overstate the benefits.

For example, it is true that the students who received the interventions in Ypsilanti, on average, went on to get more schooling than those who did not. But the average additional schooling was less than one year and over half of those who received the intervention did not finish high school.[83] While there was a big effect on teen pregnancy, those who were part of the program still had out-of-wedlock birth rates well over 50 percent.

The point here is not to belittle the accomplishments of this or other programs. The results are impressive. It is instead to highlight the extent and depth of the problem these interventions are designed to address and to temper and adjust expectations accordingly.

"The Ypsilanti experiment is a ray of hope, one that is being pursued," Wilson said, "but it remains only an attractive glimmer. Unfortunately, over eager policy makers, in their rush to do something, have magnified that ray beyond what is reasonable. We do not know why or how the Perry Preschool Program helped these sixty children in Ypsilanti or what would happen if sixty thousand youngsters in a dozen states were exposed to similar programs."[84]

Another thing to keep in mind with many early intervention programs that show promise is a phenomenon social scientists call fadeout. For many of the children who respond well at the time of the intervention, or even for a few years after, the beneficial effects gradually fade.

This should not surprise us. Once any intensive

intervention is lifted, kids will spend enormous amounts of time influenced by peers, relatives, and neighbors, the effect of which may be to undo or overwhelm the benefits of the early intervention. Further, there are certain things—such as one's genetically influenced impulses, habits, and orientations—that are difficult if not impossible for even radical outside interventions to overcome permanently.

While some early interventions can have a long and lasting effect, these successes always need to be weighed against the possibility that they cannot scale, the unintended consequences they may unleash, the enormous cost of the programs given the intensity of the interventions required, and the degree of liberty that may be sacrificed for them to have a chance of success.

Jim Manzi, who has done pioneering work studying the potential and limits of social science as a tool for shaping successful policy, notes that "those rare programs that do work usually lead to improvements that are quite modest, compared to the size of the problems they are meant to address or the dreams of the advocates."[85] This is a fair characterization of many of the early childhood interventions that have been studied to date.

It is also worth noting that the kinds of interventions Heckman and others are talking about are invasive. As Wilson has said, "serious interventions require us to trespass onto the most intimate precincts of life: the pregnant woman, the young infant, the family circle."[86] In a free society, trespassing on these areas of life carries innate hazards that should not be ignored by well-meaning policymakers.

The best and strongest "intervention" a child can receive from the crucial ages of birth to five will come from attentive, loving, biological parents. If that is absent, there may be significant limits to what public policy can achieve and we should not pretend otherwise.

STRENGTHENING INTACT FAMILIES

What of the notion of strengthening families, finding ways to encourage a child's parents to stay together and raise their children? Many policy analysts have proposed ideas with that goal in mind. Some of these ideas will strike the reader as strange or preposterous; but their advocates are accounting for the dramatic changes wrought by evolving family structure and the enormous costs that have resulted from those changes.

For example, one idea is to tax divorce.[87] Admittedly this idea will seem silly or even cruel to some readers. Divorce is almost always a miserable experience for husband, wife, and children. The writer Joseph Epstein notes that the Prophet Mohammed once described divorce as "the most detestable of all permitted things."[88] Why compound the problem by having the state impose a financial penalty?

But there is a good argument for it. People make many choices that impose costs on others, and one policy approach to address those costs is to tax those activities. As a result we put taxes on smoking and drinking to pay for the negative externalities they impose (health costs, for example). Taxing divorce could be a way to discourage it without prohibiting it, while also generating funds to cover the social and economic costs society incurs. (It is worth noting, there could be unintended consequences to divorce taxes, such as discouraging marriage in the first place.)

Another idea is to use policy to delay divorce. Under one proposal called the "The Second Chances Act," states would establish a one-year waiting period for divorce. According to researchers Leah Ward Sears and William J. Doherty, "New research shows that about 40 percent of US couples already well into the divorce process say that one or both of them are interested in the possibility of reconciliation."[89]

As figure 5.1 shows, there is some public sympathy for the idea of making divorce more difficult to obtain.

FIGURE 5.1. PERCENTAGE OF 25–60-YEAR-OLDS BELIEVING DIVORCE SHOULD BE MORE DIFFICULT TO OBTAIN, BY EDUCATION LEVEL AND DECADE

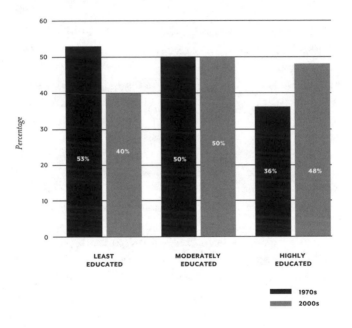

Source: State of Our Unions, "When Marriage Disappears," National Marriage Project at University of Virginia and Center for Marriage and Families at Institute for American Values, 2010.

It is interesting to see the differing directions of the trends here between least educated and highly educated Americans over time. Either way, given the widespread acceptance and normalization of divorce over several generations, it would likely take public leadership and persuasion of a kind and degree unlikely to appear soon to change laws to make divorcing much more difficult.

To address out-of-wedlock birth rates, what about ensuring that Americans, particularly the poor and middle class, have greater access to pregnancy control technologies? Sara McLanahan and her team advocate "'going to scale' with programs designed to encourage more responsible sexual behavior and by expanding access to effective contraception among individuals who might not otherwise be able to afford it."[90]

There is evidence that some public education programs aimed at increasing the use of contraception can lower pregnancy rates. But there are some good reasons to be skeptical it will make a huge dent in the problem of illegitimacy. Consider figure 5.2, which shows the percentages of young adults using birth control all the time with their sexual partners.

Barely half of highly educated single, sexually active, young Americans use birth control all the time, despite widespread family-planning education

FIGURE 5.2. PERCENTAGE OF NEVER-MARRIED YOUNG ADULTS USING BIRTH CONTROL "ALL THE TIME" WITH CURRENT OR LAST SEXUAL PARTNER, BY EDUCATION LEVEL

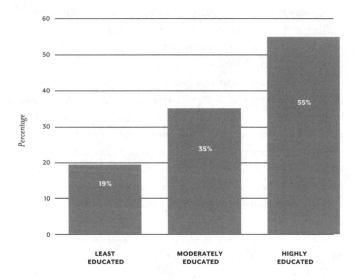

Source: State of Our Unions, "When Marriage Disappears," National Marriage Project at University of Virginia and Center for Marriage and Families at Institute for American Values, 2010.

and availability of birth-control technology. And those are the Americans best able to cope with the challenges posed by out-of-wedlock pregnancies. For Americans of little to moderate education, the percentages are even lower.

McLanahan also advocates marriage education and preparation programs that might help strengthen marriages and family life. These would include programs that

> increase union stability and father involvement in fragile families by building on marriage-education programs aimed at improving relationship skills and community-based programs aimed at raising nonresident fathers' earnings, child support payments, and parental involvement. In the case of the marriage programs, this would mean expanding services to include employment and training and mental health components. In the case of the fatherhood programs, it would mean conducting rigorous evaluations to determine what works.[91]

Some of the social scientists we cited in chapter 4 have developed ideas to address family breakdown. David Ellwood and Christopher Jencks have argued that "increasing opportunities for less skilled men seems to be an unambiguously positive step."[92]

Indeed, this was one of Moynihan's hopes when he wrote his report. The argument is that finding work opportunities for low-skilled workers would help make men more marriageable.

For example, Lawrence M. Mead of New York University has done path-breaking work examining various state programs designed to help bolster the employability of men. While many of the current programs are not well developed, Mead finds others that have had some success and could serve as a model to help men exiting the criminal justice system and those hoping to support the mothers of their children.[93]

Here, too, we should be skeptical of making large gains, given that many less-skilled men today are themselves products of broken or fragile families. As such they are lacking much of the human and social capital that makes them employable and productive. The remedial tools at our disposal to alleviate this problem are often weak. This does not mean we should abandon hope, and scholars like Mead are doing important spade work in determining the art of the possible.

Ellwood and Jencks also say that "supports for existing two parent families would seem to reduce their vulnerability."[94] This insight is behind many proposals aimed at strengthening intact families.

For example, one idea is to develop family-friendly tax policies, such as expanding child tax credits to lessen the financial burden of having and raising children. Because it is targeted and limited in scope, this is a sensible policy reform that may be able to help parents who struggle to do right by their spouses and children. It is another area worthy of study and experimentation.

THE LIMITS OF POLICY

Overall our optimism should be tempered by twin realities: the enormity of the problem and the inherent limits of social policy to affect profound change. In an astute article titled "The Limits of Policy," *New York Times* writer David Brooks noted that public policy responses to social problems, emanating from Washington or from state capitals, should be expected to accomplish only so much. He notes that the "influence of politics and policy is usually swamped by the influence of culture, ethnicity, psychology and a dozen other factors."[95]

Brooks argues that when you try to account for different economic outcomes for different people and groups over time, "you find yourself beyond narrow economic incentives and in the murky world of social capital. What matters are historical experiences, cultural attitudes, child-rearing practices, family formation patterns, expectations about the future, work ethics, and the quality of social bonds."[96] He says,

> Researchers have tried to disaggregate the influence of these soft factors and have found it nearly impossible. All we can say for sure is that different psychological, cultural, and social factors combine in myriad ways to produce different viewpoints. As a result of these different viewpoints, the average behavior is different between different ethnic and geographic groups, leading to different life outcomes.[97]

Some social changes are like a tube of toothpaste. It is easy to squeeze the toothpaste forward in one direction, significantly more difficult to reverse it and move it back into the tube from where it came. Changes in family structure are likely changes of that sort.

Any social policies designed to address social phenomena such as widespread divorce or out-of-wedlock births will likely be limited in their effectiveness, and may even be counterproductive. This should prompt us to take a step back and ask deeper and more penetrating questions about the changes in family structure.

6

HUMAN CAPITAL, SOCIAL CAPITAL, AND CHARACTER

"We are nowhere near a general theory of family change. And there we shall leave it, the question still standing: who indeed can tell us what happened to the American family?"

—Daniel Patrick Moynihan[98]

"How, I asked . . . might a government remake bad families into good ones, especially on a large scale? How might the government of a free society reshape the core values of its people and still leave them free?

—James Q. Wilson[99]

At the start of this book I argued that when Americans talk about economic problems today—poverty, income inequality, wealth disparities, unemployment, and the like—they rarely bring the enormous changes in family structure over a half century into the discussion. They are far more likely to focus on things like trade and globalization, tax policy, deregulation, immigration, "Wall Street greed," and more.

Consider the Occupy Wall Street Protests of 2011 and 2012, for example. At those rallies, and in the media coverage of them, there was a lot of emphasis on the plight of the "99 percent" versus the interests of the "1 percent."

It is difficult not to be sympathetic to poor and middle-class Americans who are having a hard time finding a job or moving up the economic ladder at a time when it is easy to find plenty of Americans doing very well economically.

In an essay for the *Los Angeles Times* at the time of the protests, I discussed some of the forces that might be driving widening disparities of wealth and income. These included immigration, technology, and globalization.

But I also included what might be the most important factor of all, namely, the collapse of the intact family. The rise in single-parent families and out-of-wedlock births—this rise in family inequality—has widened economic disparities and driven greater dependence on government for those at risk.

I pointed out that the role of soft capital—human and social capital and character—in helping a person throughout a career has become more important to economic success over the last half century. At the same time one of the chief mechanisms for inculcating that soft capital, the family, has weakened for millions of people.[100]

THINKING ABOUT CHARACTER

While not a fashionable word these days, character is important not just to individuals but also to the public interest. It is hard to think clearly about the economic challenges individuals or groups face without reference to character.

What do we mean by character? Much of it has to do with the human and social capital discussed throughout this book. For example, the late social scientist James Q. Wilson said:

> To have good character means at least two things: empathy and self-control. Empathy refers to a willingness to take importantly into account the rights, needs and feelings of others. Self-control refers to a willingness to take importantly into account the more distant consequences of present actions; to be in short somewhat future oriented rather than wholly present oriented.[101]

Empathy is a big part of a person's social capital; self-control a big part of his human capital.

Many people who find it hard, say, to hold down a job often exhibit problems of character. They have difficulty putting off present pleasures for later satisfactions so they find it hard to get to work on time or put in long hours. They find it difficult to invest in themselves by learning new skills because they have a hard time being future oriented. They simply find it hard to get along well in teams or groups of colleagues because they lack sufficient empathy.

At a dinner in Washington, DC, in 2011, I spoke with several executives at American manufacturing companies. The discussion that evening was about how to create jobs for the poor and middle class in the manufacturing sector.

Many of the representatives from manufacturing companies insisted that they had jobs they needed to fill, but they had a hard time finding workers with the requisite skills.

This lack of skills was invoked so frequently and so often, I interrupted the conversation to ask them what exactly they could not find. Was it people who could add two plus two and get four? Was it people who could do high-level calculus? What exactly was it they could not find in the labor pool?

"To be honest," said one executive, rather sheepishly, "we have a hard time finding people who can simply pass a drug test."

The skill lacking here is one of self-control, of the ability to put longer-term goals and needs ahead of short-term desires. In short, a lack of necessary character.

Let us think for a moment about the two constituent elements of character Wilson talked about—empathy and self-control—in the context of the family. The family is the first institution within which we learn about empathy, where we learn to take into account the rights, desires, and needs of others, a mother for her son, a brother for his sister, a daughter for her father, cousin for cousin, and so on.

A family is society writ small, where one learns the initial and often the deepest lessons about empathic behavior.

And think of the family and its role in regulating self-control, the ability to put immediate needs aside for longer-run interests. A healthy, well-functioning family is an extended exercise in self-control. Parents often put their immediate needs for sleep, fun, food, sex, relaxation, and more aside for the interests of their children.

Likewise, parents teach children to regulate their immediate impulses for the benefit of more distant rewards. We see this when parents insist a child do his homework or practice piano instead of watching television, run with a well-behaved crowd as opposed to a more exciting but troublesome group of peers, eat healthy food instead of the junk for which kids often ask.

Character underlies the internal determinants and controls of thought, conduct, and habit. The need to reinforce empathy and self-control among the young and adolescent is persistent and relentless. While there are other institutions that help in

this process—schools, churches, sports teams, and more—the family is the first of these and the most influential.

The family "profoundly shapes [a child's] character," Lasch tells us.[102] Today we are seeing some of what can happen to character formation when a critical character-forming institution falls apart over the course of five decades.

FAMILY AT THE CENTER

At the start of this book, I argued that many people who talk about economic topics are uncomfortable talking about the problems with the American family because discussions of the family are so often wrapped up in culture-war politics.

The problem with this reluctance is that it means our discussion of economic policy is divorced from reality. If we take family structure away from the heart of the conversation, we cannot possibly apprehend a complete picture of economic reality. Our policy choices designed to improve the future will be overly optimistic, prove limited in their effectiveness at best, and may be counterproductive at worst.

We will be like the proverbial drunks looking for car keys under the lamppost because that is where the light is shining—while the keys are somewhere else.

Bringing the family into the middle of the picture does not guarantee we will be better at solving large problems in society. After all, many of the changes that have occurred over fifty years are not just dramatic but now self-reinforcing. Correcting them will be difficult, if reverting to the way things were is even possible (or even, in some cases, desirable).

Many of the changes needed to improve family strength and cohesion might be well beyond the reach of policy and political action. They may require changes of the human heart and soul that political bureaucracies in free societies cannot effectively reach.

That may be frustrating for those who see political power as the only tool for addressing problems. But another way to look at it is as an opportunity for entrepreneurial social, religious, fraternal, and other organizations to find new ways to address the problems we are today facing.

It is worth noting that when the baleful effects of certain cultural norms, actions, and behaviors become overwhelmingly evident for all to see, societies are able to shape their cultures in a healthier direction. This has happened in the United States with the recognition of the harms of smoking. Something similar seems to be happening with recognition of the harms of obesity.

It is impossible to overstate the importance of elites in pushing cultural changes, for better and for worse. In the case of smoking and obesity, it was elites in media, politics, entertainment, philanthropy, law, science, and elsewhere who led the push for a renorming of attitudes about unhealthy behaviors.

Elites were at one time silent about the harms of smoking or actively promoted it. Today the attitude of elites is much different; many of them rail against smoking with great vigor (too much vigor, some might say!).

The point is simply that we need not be fatalistic in the face of large and dramatic changes in family structure. Just because smoking was accepted unquestioningly for a long period did not mean it would remain so forever. There is a lot of cultural inertia behind any established state of affairs. And the disintegration of the family is no different. But as the example of smoking shows, norms and attitudes can change over time once elites acknowledge the realities before them.

Either way, we cannot improve our lives together as fellow countrymen without adequately apprehending where we came from and where we may be heading. The profound transformation of American family life over the last half century will continue to have significant economic and social reverberations that will determine the kind of nation we call home for decades to come.

ENDNOTES

[1] Christopher Lasch, *Haven in a Heartless World* (New York: Basic Books, 1977), xx.

[2] Arnold Kling and Nick Schulz, *From Poverty to Prosperity* (New York: Encounter Books, 2009).

[3] Carolyn Dimitri, Ann Effland, and Neilson Conklin, "The 20th Century Transformation of U.S. Agriculture and Farm Policy" (Economic Information Bulletin no. 17, US Department of Agriculture, Washington, DC, June 2005), http://www.ers.usda.gov/publications/eib3/eib3.htm.

[4] College of Agriculture and Life Sciences, "General Facts about Agriculture," NC State University, n.d. http://www.cals.ncsu.edu/CollegeRelations/AGRICU.htm.

[5] Congressional Budget Office, "Factors Underlying the Decline in Manufacturing Employment Since 2000," *Economic and Budget Issue Brief*, December 23, 2008, http://www.cbo.gov/publication/41733.

[6] Amanda Marcotte, "Who Cares If People Don't Marry?" *Slate*'s XX Factor, December 7, 2010, http://www.slate.com/blogs/xx_factor/2010/12/07/theres_no_point_to_marriage_for_many_people.html.

[7] James T. Patterson, *Freedom Is Not Enough: The Moynihan Report and America's Struggle over Black Family Life—from LBJ to Obama* (NY: Basic Books, 2010), 188–189.

[8] *Economist*, "For Richer, for Smarter," June 23, 2011, http://www.economist.com/node/18867552.

[9] Ibid.

[10] Pew Social and Demographic Trends, "The Decline of Marriage and the Rise of New Families," Pew Research Center, November 18, 2010, http://www.pewsocialtrends.org/2010/11/18/the-decline-of-marriage-and-rise-of-new-families.

[11] Ibid.

[12] Ryan Streeter, "Marriage Rates and the Libertarian-Libertine Assault on the American Dream," RyanStreeter.com, January 2, 2012, http://ryanstreeter.com/2012/01/02/marriage-rates-and-the-libertarian-libertine-assault-on-the-american-dream.

[13] Ibid.

[14] Ruth Marcus, "The Marriage Gap Presents a Real Cost," *Washington Post*, December 17, 2011, http://www.washingtonpost.com/opinions/the-marriage-gap-presents-a-real-cost/2011/12/16/gIQAz24DzO_story.html.

[15] Charles Murray, *Coming Apart: The State of White America*, 1960–2010 (New York: Crown Forum, 2012).

[16] *Economist*, "For Richer, for Smarter."

[17] State of Our Unions, "When Marriage Disappears," National Marriage Project at University of Virginia and Center for Marriage and Families at Institute for American Values, 2010, http://stateofourunions.org/2010/when-marriage-disappears.php.

[18] George Akerlof, "Men without Children," *The Economic Journal* 108, no. 447 (March 1998): 287–309.

[19] Ibid., 288.

[20] Betsey Stevenson and Justin Wolfers, "Marriage and Divorce: Changes and Their Driving Forces" (National Bureau of Economic Research [NBER] Working Paper No. 12944, Cambridge, MA, March 2007), http://www.nber.org/papers/w12944.

[21] Brady E. Hamilton, Joyce A. Martin, and Stephanie J. Ventura, "Births: Preliminary Data for 2010," *National Vital Statistics Reports* 60, no. 2 (November 17, 2011), http://www.cdc.gov/nchs/data/nvsr/nvsr60/nvsr60_02.pdf.

[22] Jason DeParle and Sabrina Tavernise, "For Women under 30, Most Births Occur outside Marriage," *New York Times*, February 17, 2012, http://www.nytimes.com/2012/02/18/us/for-women-under-30-most-births-occur-outside-marriage.html?pagewanted=all.

[23] State of Our Unions, "When Marriage Disappears."

[24] Jason DeParle and Sabrina Tavernise, "For Women under 30, Most Births Occur outside Marriage."

[25] Sara McLanahan, Irwin Garfinkel, Ronald B. Mincy, and Elizabeth Donahue, "Introducing the Issue," *Fragile Families* 20, no. 2 (Fall 2010), http://www.futureofchildren.org/futureofchildren/publications/journals/article/index.xml?journalid=73&articleid=528&sectionid=3635&submit.

[26] Jason DeParle and Sabrina Tavernise, "For Women under 30, Most Births Occur outside Marriage."

[27] Pew Research Center, "The Decline of Marriage and Rise of New Families," *Social and Demographic Trends Report*, November 18, 2010, part II, http://www.pewsocialtrends.org/2010/11/18/the-decline-of-marriage-and-rise-of-new-families/2.

[28] Scott Hankins and Mark Hoekstra, "Lucky in Life, Unlucky in Love? The Effect of Random Income Shocks on Marriage and Divorce," *Journal of Human Resources* 46, no. 2 (Spring 2011): 403–26.

[29] State of Our Unions, "When Marriage Disappears."

[30] Charles Murray, "Why Economics Can't Explain Our Cultural Divide," *Wall Street Journal*, March 18, 2012, http://www.aei.org/article/society-and-culture/why-economics-cant-explain-our-cultural-divide.

[31] "Church Attendance Is Declining," The Heritage Foundation, familyfacts.org, n.d., http://www.familyfacts.org/charts/620/church-attendance-is-declining.

[32] Mark Bauerlein, "An Unnatural Habitat: The Separate Lives of Adolescents," in *Acculturated*, ed. Naomi Schaefer Riley and Christine Rosen (West Conshohocken, PA: Templeton Press, 2011), 61.

[33] James S. Coleman, "The Adolescent Society," *Education Next* (Winter 2006), http://media.hoover.org/sites/default/files/documents/ednext20061_40.pdf, taken from James Coleman, "Academic Achievement and the Structure of Competition," *Harvard Education Review* 29, no. 4 (Fall 1959).

[34] Mark Bauerlein, "An Unnatural Habitat: The Separate Lives of Adolescents," 67.

[35] Jason Collins, "IQ Externalities," *Evolving Economics*, December 22, 2011, http://www.jasoncollins.org/2011/12/iq-externalities.

[36] Ron Haskins and Isabel Sawhill, *Creating an Opportunity Society* (Washington, DC: Brookings Institution Press, 2009).

[37] Sara McLanahan and Gary Sandefur, *Growing Up with a Single Parent: What Hurts, What Helps* (Cambridge, MA: Harvard College, 1994), 1.

[38] Ibid., 2.

39 David T. Ellwood and Christopher Jencks, "The Spread of Single-Parent Families in the United States Since 1960" (working paper, John F. Kennedy School of Government, Harvard University, October 2002), http://www.hks.harvard.edu/inequality/Seminar/Papers/ElwdJnck.pdf.

40 The Bendhcim-Thoman Center for Research on Child Wellbeing and Columbia Population Research Center, "Fragile Families and Child Wellbeing Study," Princeton University and Columbia University, n.d., www.fragilefamilies.princeton.edu.

41 Michael S. Christian, "Human Capital Accounting in the United States: Context, Measurement, and Application" (working paper, Wisconsin Center for Education Research, July 2011), http://www.bea.gov/papers/pdf/human_capital_accounting_in_the_united_states.pdf.

42 McLanahan and Sandefur, *Growing Up With a Single Parent: What Hurts, What Helps*, 8.

43 Christopher Lasch, *Haven in a Heartless World*, 3.

44 Ibid., 3–4.

45 Ibid., 4.

46 R. R. Reno, "The Preferential Option for the Poor,"

First Things, June/July 2011, http://www.firstthings.com/article/2011/05/the-preferential-option-for-the-poor.

[47] James J. Heckman, "The American Family in Black and White: A Post-Racial Strategy for Improving Skills to Promote Equality" (NBER Working Paper No. 16841, Cambridge, MA, March 2011), www.nber.org/papers/w16841.

[48] James J. Heckman, "Schools, Skills, and Synapses" (discussion paper no. 3515, Institute for the Study of Labor, Bonn, Germany, May 2008), http://ftp.iza.org/dp3515.pdf.

[49] Roy F. Baumeister and John Tierney, *Willpower: Rediscovering the Greatest Human Strength* (London: Penguin, 2011), 207.

[50] Arnold Kling, "Willpower," *EconLib*, September 15, 2011, http://econlog.econlib.org/archives/2011/09/willpower.html.

[51] Thomas DeLeire and Leonard M. Lopoo, *Family Structure and the Economic Mobility of Children* (Washington, DC: Economic Mobility Project, Pew Charitable Trust, April 2010), 5, http://www.economicmobility.org/assets/pdfs/Family_Structure.pdf.

[52] Ibid., 4.

[53] Ibid., 4.

[54] Ibid., 2.

[55] Pew Research Center, "The Decline of Marriage and Rise of New Families," part II.

[56] Ibid.

[57] Alex Moe and Domenico Montanaro, "Fact Check: Santorum Claims It's Cheaper to Be Single, but Is It?" *First Read,* October 3, 2011, http://firstread.msnbc.msn.com/news/2011/10/03/8127377-fact-check-santorum-claims-its-cheaper-to-be-single-but-is-it.

[58] Nicholas D. Kristof, "The White Underclass," *New York Times,* February 8, 2012, http://www.nytimes.com/2012/02/09/opinion/kristof-the-decline-of-white-workers.html?_r=2&hp.

[59] Daniel Patrick Moynihan, *The Negro Family: The Case for National Action* (Washington, DC: US Department of Labor, Office of Policy Planning and Research, March 1965), http://www.dol.gov/oasam/programs/history/webid-meynihan.htm.

[60] James T. Patterson, *Freedom Is Not Enough,* 5.

[61] Daniel Patrick Moynihan, *The Negro Family*.

[62] Kay Hymowitz, "The Black Family: 40 Years of Lies," *City Journal* (Summer 2005), http://www.city-journal.org/html/15_3_black_family.html.

[63] Daniel Patrick Moynihan, *The Negro Family*.

[64] Ibid.

[65] Ibid.

[66] Steven F. Hayward, "Do It for the Children, for Real," *Powerline*, October 17, 2011, http://www.powerlineblog.com/archives/2011/10/do-it-for-the-children-for-real.php.

[67] Steven F. Hayward, *The Age of Reagan: The Fall of the Old Liberal Order; 1964–1980* (New York: Three Rivers Press, 2001).

[68] Ibid., 93.

[69] Daniel Patrick Moynihan, *The Negro Family*.

[70] James T. Patterson, *Freedom Is Not Enough*, 195.

[71] Ibid.

[72] Peter Wehner, "Walk Back to the Right Road to Marriage and Parenthood," *Commentary*, February 21, 2012, http://eppc.org/publications/pubID.4679/pub_detail.asp.

[73] David Greenberg, "Essay; No Exit," *New York Times*, March 20, 2011, http://query.nytimes.com/gst/fullpage.html?res=9E03E0DD133EF933A15750C0A9679D8B63&pagewanted=all.

[74] David T. Ellwood and Christopher Jencks, "The Spread of Single-Parent Families in the United States since 1960," 33.

[75] George Will, in Arthur C. Brooks, Charles Murray, and George Will, "The Sinatra of Social Science," *The American*, January 6, 2012, http://www.american.com/archive/2012/january/the-sinatra-of-social-science.

[76] Keith A. Owens, "Society Shouldn't Try to Hide behind Fuzzy 'Family Values,'" *Sun Sentinel*, November 24, 1990, http://articles.sun-sentinel.com/1990-11-24/news/9002270229_1_family-values-traditional-family-moral-values.

[77] James Heckman, "Stimulating the Young," *The American*, August 7, 2009, http://american.com/archive/2009/august/stimulating-the-young/?searchterm=heckman.

[78] Ibid.

[79] Ibid.

[80] Jonathan Cohn, "The Two Year Window," *The New Republic*, November 9, 2011, http://www.tnr.com/article/economy/magazine/97268/the-two-year-window?page=0,0.

[81] James Heckman, "Stimulating the Young."

[82] James Q. Wilson, *On Character: Essays by James Q. Wilson* (Washington, DC: AEI Press, 1995), 51.

[83] Texas Youth Commission, "Prevention Summary" of L. J. Schweinhart and D. P. Weikart (eds.), *Significant Benefits: The High/Scope Perry Preschool Study through Age 27* (Ypsilanti, MI: High/Scope Press, 1993), ch. 10, http://web.archive. org/web/20050212205829/http://www.tyc.state.tx.us/ prevention/hiscope.html.

[84] James Q. Wilson, *On Character*, 51.

[85] Jim Manzi, "What Social Science Does—and Doesn't—Know," *City Journal* 20, no. 3 (Summer 2010), http://www. city-journal.org/2010/20_3_social-science.html.

[86] James Q. Wilson, *On Character*, 50.

[87] R. R. Reno, "The Preferential Option for the Poor."

[88] Joseph Epstein, *Divorced in America: Marriage in an Age of Possibility* (New York: Dutton, 1974).

[89] Maggie Gallagher, "A Modest Proposal to Reduce Unnecessary Divorce," *Public Discourse*, The Witherspoon Institute, October 27, 2011, http://www.thepublicdiscourse. com/2011/10/4203.

[90] Princeton University and The Brookings Institution, "Fragile Families," *The Future of Children* 20, no. 2 (Fall 2010), 14, http://futureofchildren.org/futureofchildren/ publications/docs/20_02_FullJournal.pdf.

[91] Ibid., 16.

[92] David T. Ellwood and Christopher Jencks, "The Spread of Single-Parent Families in the United States since 1960" (Kennedy School of Government Working Paper No. RWP04-008, Harvard University, Cambridge, MA, February 26, 2004), 34, http://papers.ssrn.com/sol3/papers.cfm?abstract_id=517662.

[93] Lawrence M. Mead, *Expanding Work Programs for Poor Men* (Washington, DC: AEI Press, May 2011).

[94] David T. Ellwood and Christopher Jencks, "The Spread of Single-Parent Families in the United States since 1960," 34.

[95] David Brooks, "The Limits of Policy," *New York Times*, May 3, 2010, http://www.nytimes.com/2010/05/04/opinion/04brooks.html.

[96] Ibid.

[97] Ibid.

[98] James T. Patterson, *Freedom Is Not Enough*, 189.

[99] James Q. Wilson, *American Politics Then and Now and Other Essays* (Washington, DC: AEI Press, 2010), 46.

[100] Nick Schulz, "Three Inconvenient Truths for Occupy Wall Street," *Los Angeles Times*, November 30, 2011, http://articles.latimes.com/2011/nov/30/opinion/la-oe-schulz-occupy-20111130.

[101] James Q. Wilson, *On Character*, 5.

[102] Christopher Lasch, *Haven in a Heartless World*, 3.

ABOUT THE AUTHOR

Nick Schulz was the DeWitt Wallace Fellow at AEI and editor-in-chief of American.com, AEI's online magazine focusing on business, economics, and public affairs. He now works in the private sector. He is the co-author with Arnold Kling of *From Poverty to Prosperity: Intangible Assets, Hidden Liabilities, and the Lasting Triumph Over Scarcity* (2009).